Journeying
through Advent
with **New Daylight**

BRF

The Bible Reading Fellowship
15 The Chambers, Vineyard
Abingdon OX14 3FE
brf.org.uk

The Bible Reading Fellowship (BRF) is a Registered Charity (233280)

ISBN 978 0 85746 967 0
First published 2020; reprinted 2020
10 9 8 7 6 5 4 3 2 1
All rights reserved

Acknowledgements
Scripture quotations marked with the following acronyms are taken from the version shown. Where no acronym is given, the quotation is taken from the same version as the headline reference. NRSV: The New Revised Standard Version of the Bible, Anglicised edition, copyright © 1989, 1995 by the Division of Christian Education of the National Council of the Churches of Christ in the United States of America. Used by permission. All rights reserved. NIV: The Holy Bible, New International Version (Anglicised edition) copyright © 1979, 1984, 2011 by Biblica. Used by permission of Hodder & Stoughton Publishers, a Hachette UK company. All rights reserved. 'NIV' is a registered trademark of Biblica. UK trademark number 1448790. MSG: The Message, copyright © 1993, 1994, 1995, 1996, 2000, 2001, 2002 by Eugene H. Peterson. Used by permission of NavPress. All rights reserved. Represented by Tyndale House Publishers, Inc. NLT: The Holy Bible, New Living Translation, copyright © 1996, 2004, 2007, 2013. Used by permission of Tyndale House Publishers, Inc., Carol Stream, Illinois 60188. All rights reserved. TNIV: The Holy Bible, Today's New International Version, copyright © 2004 by Biblica. Used by permission of Hodder & Stoughton Publishers, a division of Hodder Headline Ltd. All rights reserved. 'TNIV' is a registered trademark of International Bible Society. NASB: The New American Standard Bible®, Copyright © 1960, 1962, 1963, 1968, 1971, 1972, 1973, 1975, 1977, 1995 by The Lockman Foundation. Used by permission (www.Lockman.org). GNT: The Good News Bible published by The Bible Societies/ HarperCollins Publishers Ltd, UK © American Bible Society 1966, 1971, 1976, 1992, used with permission. ESV: The Holy Bible, English Standard Version, published by HarperCollins Publishers, © 2001 Crossway Bibles, a division of Good News Publishers. Used by permission. All rights reserved.

Every effort has been made to trace and contact copyright owners for material used in this resource. We apologise for any inadvertent omissions or errors, and would ask those concerned to contact us so that full acknowledgement can be made in the future.

A catalogue record for this book is available from the British Library

Printed and bound in the UK by Zenith Media NP4 0DQ

Contents

About the contributors

David Winter is one of the UK's most popular and long-established Christian writers and broadcasters. He has written many books, including *At the End of the Day* (2013) and *Heaven's Morning* (2016) for BRF. He was also a regular contributor to Radio 4's *Thought for the Day* from 1989 to 2012.

Steve Aisthorpe is the Church of Scotland's mission development worker for the Highlands and Islands. He was previously executive director of the International Nepal Fellowship and contributed to BRF's *Holy Habits Bible Reflections* and *Group Studies*. He is an enthusiastic coach and retreat leader.

Amy Boucher Pye is a writer, speaker and retreat leader who runs the *Woman Alive* book club. She's the author of the award-winning *Finding Myself in Britain* (Authentic, 2015) and *The Living Cross* (BRF, 2016) and has an MA in Christian spirituality. Find her at **amyboucherpye.com**.

Andy John has been Bishop of Bangor since 2008. He has a particular interest in the relationship between the gospel and culture (especially art and music).

Margaret Cundiff, who died in 2011, was one of the first women to be ordained in 1994. A priest, writer, broadcaster and chaplain, she was also a member of the Third Order of Franciscans.

Introduction

SALLY WELCH

Last year my parish church put on its first ever Christmas Tree Festival. Over 30 organisations and businesses, ranging from the local cafe to the Bowls Club, the Refugee Action Committee to our marvellous honey farmer took part. Christmas trees lined the nave and the chancel, and hundreds of people visited to admire the decorations and vote for their favourite tree. Concerts, parties and a final 'Songs of Praise' event added the finishing touches to a busy and successful weekend. Money was raised for the church roof, connections were established with local groups and people came and celebrated the start of Christmas with their local church.

So why then did I feel slightly unsettled by it all? Why did I have a sense that somehow something was missing? On reflection I realised that the Christmas Tree Festival, with its joy and its colour, its singing and its hospitality, had driven a great big, tinsel-bedecked truck right through our preparations for the birth of the Saviour of the world!

Advent is a sombre time in the church calendar – a season when flowers do not decorate churches, the liturgical colour is a mournful purple and the readings look forward with a degree of apprehension as well as anticipation. While all the rest of the world is covering itself in glitter and sparkle, immersed in an orgy of spending and over-indulging, the church alone stands sober and still, determinedly counter-cultural. And it is right that this is so. By doing so, we can offer that most precious gift of all – that of time: time to pause and reflect on the nature of the event that changed the course of the world forever; time to decide how we will respond to this gift at once so small and yet with such potential; time to turn and face the world with love and hope, offering to others what has been offered to us with such generosity.

My prayer for us this Advent is that we use the time we have been given in this spacious season to look forward with hope to the kingdom which is God is preparing for us – a kingdom of righteousness, justice and peace, where our tears have no place because the King of love has wiped them all away, where the transformation first begun by a baby born in a stable is finally and completely realised and the world unites to sing.

This theme of hope is explored lovingly by many of the writers in this study guide. One of *New Daylight*'s favourite writers, David Winter, begins by looking forward with the prophets as he explores the Advent antiphons, those names of Christ which echo through the centuries, bringing their promise of hope and justice. These names are translated into principles in the second and third letters of John, and Steve Aisthorpe shares with us practical examples of living in truth and love.

As we approach the shortest night, Amy Boucher Pye encourages us to look through God's eyes as the light of his love shines into the darkest corners of our world. That light is, of course, Christ – the light of all peoples, a light no darkness can overcome, and Andy John brings our Advent studies to a close with his investigation into that most classic of Christmas passages, the first verses of the gospel of John. Finally Margaret Cundiff invites us to greet the new year with hope as we explore the reassurance and faith offered to us in some of our favourite psalms: 'Surely goodness and mercy shall follow me all the days of my life, and I shall dwell in the house of the Lord my whole life long.'

With every blessing this Advent season

Sally Annwelch

How to use this material in a group

This material can be used in a number of different ways by all sorts of groups. If your group is already meeting, it can provide the scripture or discussion input, reminding group members of the 'alternative Advent' to shopping, cooking and other preparations for Christmas. It can also form the basis for a weekly Advent group. Similar to a Lent group, this can provide members with space for reflection during a busy time and perhaps offer a springboard to a year-round study group.

If a new group is beginning, it is a good idea to include refreshments with each meeting – some groups find an evening meal with discussion round the table very popular, while others feel that drinks and biscuits or cake are more appropriate. This kind of hospitality can break down barriers and introduce people to each other in a relaxed way, which in turn will lead to a livelier, more fruitful discussion.

Remember to provide prospective members of the group with booklets well before the beginning of Advent. The reflections begin on 1 December and continue to Epiphany on 6 January.

The group leader may or may not also be the group host. Either or both of these roles may be fixed for the whole of Advent or rotate among the group.

If the group leader and host are different people, they should liaise beforehand to ensure arrangements are in place, the time and date are fixed and refreshments are available.

Introduction Make sure each person has a copy of the booklet and that spares are available for those who do not. Introduce newcomers to the group and make them feel welcome. Remind everyone that they do not have to contribute to the discussion if they don't want to, but that conversation will be livelier if they do!

Opening prayer Use a prayer within the traditions of the group; this will help put people at ease, and those who are familiar with the traditions will lend confidence to those who are not. A song or hymn can be sung.

Discussion If the group is large, split into twos or threes to discuss reactions to the week's reflections. Allow time for each person to share, if they wish. If discussion is slow to start, suggest that each member offers one word or sentence that sums up their reaction.

Forum As one group, try to discern some themes that are common to most members. If it helps, write these down and circulate them among the group.

Reflection Each set of study questions relates to one day's reading. You may wish to read that day's reflection aloud together first. Study the group questions, and spend some time in silence so that individuals can reflect on the theme personally. Come together to discuss the questions. Again, if the group is large it is helpful to split into smaller groups.

Plenary The leader draws together the themes arising from the discussion, and sees whether they mirror those from the week's reflections. Again, these can be noted for later distribution.

Prayer It can be helpful to begin your prayer time with silence, in order to meditate on the results of the discussion. This can be followed by open prayer. Be flexible, allowing time for each person to contribute if they wish.

Closing prayer.

The Advent antiphons

DAVID WINTER

The call of Moses

Exodus 3:3–6 (NRSV)

Then Moses said, 'I must turn aside and look at this great sight, and see why the bush is not burned up.' When the Lord saw that he had turned aside to see, God called to him out of the bush, 'Moses, Moses!' And he said, 'Here I am.' Then he said, 'Come no closer! Remove the sandals from your feet, for the place on which you are standing is holy ground.' He said further, 'I am the God of your father, the God of Abraham, the God of Isaac, and the God of Jacob.' And Moses hid his face, for he was afraid to look at God.

Reflection

The Israelites were slaves in Egypt, oppressed by cruel task-masters and forced to build Pharaoh's treasure houses. In their suffering, they had cried out to God and he had heard their cries. Now, in an astonishing sequence of events – which began with the birth of Moses and culminates here, at Mount Horeb – God puts into operation his great plan to rescue his people and bring them to their promised land.

This moment at the burning bush is a turning point not just for the Hebrew people, but also in the whole story of God's dealings with the human race. The voice that called Moses was none other than that of Yahweh, the eternal, personal, all-powerful 'God of Abraham, Isaac and Jacob'. From that moment, the destiny of the Hebrew people changed. Redemption, freedom, the law, covenant and promises of God would all be theirs. Ahead lay rivers to cross and tests that they could not have imagined, but beyond it all lay the promised land, 'flowing with milk and honey'. On that journey, their God would be with them every step of the way.

What was true for them, the people of the old covenant, is just as true for us, the people of the new one. Our God is not helpless or insensitive to our needs; he is silently planning for us in love. That is the truth of Bethlehem, but it is also the great Advent truth. With God, nothing is ever finally hopeless.

O come, O come, Adonai, who in thy glorious majesty from Sinai's mountain, clothed in awe, gavest thy folk the ancient law. Rejoice, rejoice! Emmanuel shall come to thee, O Israel.

DAVID WINTER

The stock of Jesse

Isaiah 11:1–3 (NRSV)

A shoot shall come out from the stock of Jesse, and a branch shall grow out of his roots. The spirit of the Lord shall rest on him, the spirit of wisdom and understanding, the spirit of counsel and might, the spirit of knowledge and the fear of the Lord. His delight shall be in the fear of the Lord. He shall not judge by what his eyes see, or decide by what his ears hear.

Reflection

Years ago, when I was rector of a Cotswold village, there was a carving of a Jesse tree in the north aisle of our beautiful Norman church. Its idea was, of course, based on these verses – the 'shoot' from the 'stock of Jesse' was his descendant, the father of the shepherd boy David, who became Israel's greatest king. As we look ahead to Christmas, the connection with Bethlehem becomes obvious, because there a 'shoot' from Jesse's stock was born – Jesus, a descendant of David. So Christians have always read this passage as a prophecy of the birth of the Messiah, Jesus.

These words emphasise the role of the Holy Spirit in the character and life of Jesus. His first public utterance, in the synagogue at Nazareth, began with words from this same prophet:

'The Spirit of the Lord is upon me' (Luke 4:18). Here, we are reminded of some of the Spirit's particular gifts – wisdom, understanding, counsel, might, knowledge and fear (in the sense of reverence).

'Wisdom', in the language of the Bible, is much more than a concept or abstract principle. God is pure wisdom and Jesus was wisdom incarnate – perfect wisdom in human form. The Old Testament asserts several times that 'the fear of the Lord… is wisdom' (for example, Job 28:28), but only in Jesus did that reverence of the Father reach perfection. His wisdom gave him understanding, in the deepest sense, and also knowledge – he 'knew all people… for he himself knew what was in everyone' (John 2:24–25). That in turn gave him the gift of counsel, for when he spoke it was on the basis of knowledge, not guesswork.

O come, thou root of Jesse! Draw the quarry from the lion's claw; from those dread caverns of the grave, from nether hell thy people save. Rejoice, rejoice! Emmanuel shall come to thee, O Israel.

DAVID WINTER

Righteousness and justice

Isaiah 11:3–5 (NRSV)

His delight shall be in the fear of the Lord. He shall not judge by what his eyes see, or decide by what his ears hear; but with righteousness he shall judge the poor, and decide with equity for the meek of the earth; he shall strike the earth with the rod of his mouth, and with the breath of his lips he shall kill the wicked. Righteousness shall be the belt around his waist, and faithfulness the belt around his loins.

Reflection

'Righteousness' and 'faithfulness' are to be the two distinguishing virtues of the Messiah. 'Righteousness' simply means 'doing what is right', which means, in effect, doing what God requires of us. It is not only one of the most common words in the Old Testament, but also on the lips of Jesus. He himself came to 'fulfil all righteousness' (Matthew 3:15) and called his followers to 'strive first' for God's righteousness, to make it a priority (Matthew 6:33). Indeed, he warned them that 'unless your righteousness exceeds that of the scribes and Pharisees, you will never enter the kingdom of heaven' (Matthew 5:20). The righteousness of the scribes and Pharisees was concerned with ritual, law and outward show. True righteousness is concerned with behaviour – what we do and what we are.

This is a picture of God's righteous one, and it is interesting that this behaviour necessarily involves not only doing good (exercising faithfulness and doing what God requires) but also opposing evil. Sometimes we shy away from the latter – 'Who am I,' we ask ourselves, 'to denounce what is wrong in others when I am only too conscious of my own failings?' Yet the two are indivisible. Sometimes our role is to do what is right ourselves. Sometimes our role is to oppose what is wrong, whoever is responsible for it. This is not a matter of personal whim, either, deciding on the basis of what my eyes see or my ears hear, but on the basis of God's standards – 'righteousness and equity', fairness, justice. That is God's model and we can see it best in Jesus, and will see it again when he comes as judge.

Son of David, you stand as a sign among the nations; rulers will keep silence before you for whom the nations long; come and save us without delay.

DAVID WINTER

True security

Isaiah 22:21–23 (NRSV)

And [I] will clothe [Eliakim] with your robe and bind your sash on him. I will commit your authority to his hand, and he shall be a father to the inhabitants of Jerusalem and to the house of Judah. I will place on his shoulder the key of the house of David; he shall open, and no one shall shut; he shall shut, and no one shall open. I will fasten him like a peg in a secure place, and he will become a throne of honour to his ancestral house.

Reflection

It is often said that religion is a crutch. Well, if you've broken your ankle you're grateful for one!

Where human beings are concerned, most of us have moments of insecurity and fear when we feel the need for some source of comfort and reassurance beyond ourselves. In this powerful prophecy from Isaiah, we hear God's warning to the faithless steward Shebna that his responsibilities will be stripped from him and given to 'my servant Eliakim', who would then be a father to the nation and bear final responsibility in making judgement (using the 'key' of authority to open and shut the kingdom). In this way, he would restore the Davidic tradition, which recent events had sorely tarnished. These words are echoed in Jesus' commission to Peter and the apostles (Matthew 16:19), who in his name would open (or close) the gates of the kingdom of heaven by preaching the gospel and calling for a response.

Eliakim (who was not to be king, but the king's steward) would also be a secure 'peg' on which could be hung all the honours of the house of David. Some responsibility! I think this passage is included in Advent readings because it speaks of the enormous expectations attached to the tradition of David, expectations that could only be fulfilled when Jesus, the greatest son of David, came to us. In him is true security, a safe 'peg' on which to hang our anxieties, and he is the one who unlocked, in his death and resurrection, the kingdom, not of David but of heaven itself.

O come, thou Lord of David's key! The royal door fling wide and free; safeguard for us the heavenward road, and bar the way to death's abode. Rejoice, rejoice! Emmanuel shall come to thee, O Israel.

DAVID WINTER

Sceptre and star

Numbers 24:15–17 (NRSV)

So [Balaam] uttered his oracle, saying: 'The oracle of Balaam son of Beor, the oracle of the man whose eye is clear, the oracle of one who hears the words of God, and knows the knowledge of the Most High, who sees the vision of the Almighty, who falls down, but with his eyes uncovered: I see him, but not now; I behold him, but not near – a star shall come out of Jacob, and a sceptre shall rise out of Israel; it shall crush the borderlands of Moab, and the territory of all the Shethites.'

Reflection

Balaam is a strange figure of a prophet in this story, because he was not a Jew, a man of the covenant, but one of the mysterious and honoured 'God-fearers' who feature a good deal in the Old Testament. He claimed to speak what 'the LORD' – the capital letters in most translations tell us that he was referring to *Yahweh* – was telling him. This despite being urged by the enemy King Balak to curse the Israelites.

Far from cursing them, Balaam offered this remarkable oracle – a visionary prophecy. In it he is given a vision of 'the Almighty' – perceived, apparently, while he was lying on the ground but with his eyes open. He saw a person who was yet to be ('I see him, but not now'), a shining star, bringing light and fulfilling promises, and a sceptre, denoting kingship. To the Jewish people, this has always spoken of the great King David, who would lead the nation into its glory days. To Christians down the ages, it has been a promise of one even greater than David, through his descendant. David was always seen as coming from and uniting Israel and 'Jacob' (Judea).

For us today, it is a prophetic word about the one who came and is yet to come. He will indeed come with authority, but also as a bright and shining light, a star to lighten the cosmic scene. A star led the magi to Bethlehem. Perhaps an even brighter star will lead us eventually into the kingdom of heaven.

O come, O come, thou dayspring bright! Pour on our souls thy healing light; dispel the long night's lingering gloom, and pierce the shadows of the tomb. Rejoice, rejoice! Emmanuel shall come to thee, O Israel.

DAVID WINTER

Freedom and release

Jeremiah 30:7–9 (NRSV)

Alas! that day is so great there is none like it; it is a time of distress for Jacob; yet he shall be rescued from it. On that day, says the Lord of hosts, I will break the yoke from off his neck, and I will burst his bonds, and strangers shall no more make a servant of him. But they shall serve the Lord their God and David their king, whom I will raise up for them.

Reflection

We move on, in this panorama of prophecy, to the great prophet Jeremiah. He was not a man to pull punches! Having laid it on the line for the people of Judea (Jacob) – they were going into captivity, for their sin and wilfulness – he now assures them that God does not forget his covenant promises. The day of punishment will be dreadful indeed, but there will also be a wonderful day of redemption and freedom.

When that day comes, it will not be the bringer of a partial or conditional release. The yoke of foreign bondage will indeed be broken. The prisoners' chains will be snapped; they will no longer be slaves and captives. However, this is not simply release from evil – it is delivery into a great good. At last they will be free to serve God and live under the reign of someone the prophet calls 'David'.

All through these prophecies, the name recurs. Clearly this is no longer the historical King David, who reigned and then died, leaving only an honoured memory. This is the whole Davidic principle, the idea that God would one day send his people a king like David – just, victorious, God-fearing. Thus, the people awaited a literal descendant of the great king, but one who would be imbued with divine power – a messiah indeed.

They did not know it then, but the event would be delayed for several centuries yet, and I suppose we could say that we still wait, expectantly, for its complete fulfilment. David's 'son' came to set us free, and he will come again to bring in that godly reign of justice and peace promised so long ago.

O come, desire of nations! Show thy kingly reign on earth below; thou cornerstone, uniting all, restore the ruin of our fall. Rejoice, rejoice! Emmanuel shall come to thee, O Israel.

DAVID WINTER

The God who comes to save us

Jeremiah 30:10–11a (NRSV)

But as for you, have no fear, my servant Jacob, says the Lord, and do not be dismayed, O Israel; for I am going to save you from far away, and your offspring from the land of their captivity. Jacob shall return and have quiet and ease, and no one shall make him afraid. For I am with you, says the Lord, to save you.

Reflection

One of the great themes of the Bible is that God is with us, as well as above us. Most religions recognise the power and otherness of God, but Judaism and Christianity are unique in the concept of God being near us, with us. In the Old Testament, God heard his people's cries and appeared to Moses at the burning bush. He explained that he had 'come down to deliver them from the Egyptians' (Exodus 3:8). In fact, Moses and Aaron were to be the human instruments of that rescue, but they were aware of God's presence with them and so were the Israelites as they set out across the Red Sea on their journey to the promised land. The signs of that presence were the pillar of cloud by day and of fire by night.

At other times, too, God drew near to his people, sometimes in moments of crisis and sometimes to encourage and support them. Isaiah speaks of a baby who would be born and called 'Immanuel', which means 'God is with us' (Isaiah 7:14).

Here, Jeremiah also promises the people that the Lord would be 'with them to save them' in their time of fear and distress. In other words, this is no distant, remote deity, firing off commands from a far-away heaven, but a God who comes to his people. That is also a great theme of the New Testament. Jesus is described as 'the one who is to come' (Luke 7:19), the promised 'Emmanuel' (Matthew 1:23). In our earthly journey he will be with us to the end of time (Matthew 28:20), but he also says that he will come again to bring in the final reign of God and all the blessings of his kingdom.

Jesus, you are our Emmanuel, the hope of the nations and their Saviour; come and save us, O Lord.

DAVID WINTER

Week 1: Group study questions

Righteousness and justice (3 December)

1 Consider this picture of the coming Messiah. What
   strikes you about it?

2 What do you think is meant by the words, 'He shall not
   judge by what his eyes see, or decide by what his ears
   hear'?

3 How can we, as flawed humans, perceive what is right
   and what is wrong? We may face situations where we
   are uncertain how to act – note these for prayer later.

4 At the start of Advent, a time of reflection and
   preparation, how 'righteous' do you truly feel? Share
   your thoughts in pairs or reflect in silence.

5 What can we commit to doing as a group that promotes
   righteousness and justice at this season?

2 and 3 John

STEVE AISTHORPE

Truth that transforms

2 John 1–4 (NIV)

The elder, To the lady chosen by God and to her children, whom I love in the truth – and not I only, but also all who know the truth – because of the truth, which lives in us and will be with us for ever: Grace, mercy and peace from God the Father and from Jesus Christ, the Father's Son, will be with us in truth and love. It has given me great joy to find some of your children walking in the truth, just as the Father commanded us.

Reflection

Considering how little ink was required to write this letter, it is incredible how much has been spent debating to whom it was addressed. Some suggest that it was written to a woman and her family, but most scholars see this as a letter to a church. So, Eugene Peterson begins his translation, 'My dear congregation' (MSG). This understanding makes 'the children' members of that local Christian community. John had met some of them and was overjoyed to find them 'walking in the truth' (v. 4).

Truth is the dominant theme in John's opening remarks. He mentions it five times in four short verses. The truth (God's actions in history and their significance) can be 'known' (v. 1), but not in the way we might know cold facts. Rather, the truth is to 'live in us' (v. 2), changing us from the inside out.

As in many places throughout the UK, churches in my local city work together to train and mobilise teams of street pastors. These teams walk the city centre in the early hours, engaging with people, caring and listening. Recently, the project coordinator told me that the people they meet are generally less concerned with whether the claims of Christianity are true or not and more in whether 'it works'. They want to see truth lived out.

John challenges the contemporary notion that truth is a matter of opinion and he clearly expects that what we know should be reflected in how we live. Time and again, the actions of Jesus gave credibility to his words; over and over his words explained his actions.

Jesus both proclaimed the truth and demonstrated that 'it works'. He asks that we do likewise.

STEVE AISTHORPE

The principal principle

2 John 5–6 (NIV)

And now, dear lady, I am not writing you a new command but one we have had from the beginning. I ask that we love one another. And this is love: that we walk in obedience to his commands. As you have heard from the beginning, his command is that you walk in love.

Reflection

Whether a simple shack or a grand design, a building starts with its foundation. So John, a master builder of disciples and churches, before addressing a particular peril facing this church, checks the groundwork. There is nothing new here, only a reminder, but it is so crucial, so vital, that even in such a short note, he dare not exclude it. It is the most uncomplicated yet also the most demanding of commandments: 'love one another' (v. 5). Whatever challenges face a church, reinforcing this foundation is always the right starting point.

In his first letter, John made the astonishing declaration that 'God is love' (1 John 4:8). It reveals the very essence of God's character. In the light of this, it is unsurprising that 'God in flesh', Jesus Christ, and his first followers should insist that love must be the hallmark and touchstone of his people (John 13:34; 1 John 3:23).

How can we grow in love? At times, Christ's expectations of his church seem unattainable. Alone we cannot change, 'but the fruit of the Spirit is love' (Galatians 5:22). Archbishop William Temple illustrated it this way: 'It is no good giving me a play like *Hamlet* and telling me to write a play like that. Shakespeare could do it – I can't. And it is no good showing me a life like the life of Jesus and telling me to live a life like that. Jesus could do it – I can't. But if the genius of Shakespeare could come and live in me, then I could write plays like his. And if the Spirit of Christ could come into me, then I could live a life like his' (quoted in John Stott, *Basic Christianity*, 1958). God's love has been poured out into our hearts through the Holy Spirit (Romans 5:5).

**God of love, please cultivate more of
your love in me. Amen**

STEVE AISTHORPE

True or false?

2 John 7–11 (NIV)

Many deceivers, who do not acknowledge Jesus Christ as coming in the flesh, have gone out into the world. Any such person is the deceiver and the antichrist. Watch out that you do not lose what we have worked for, but that you may be rewarded fully. Anyone who runs ahead and does not continue in the teaching of Christ does not have God; whoever continues in the teaching has both the Father and the Son. If anyone comes to you and does not bring this teaching, do not take them into your house or welcome them. Anyone who welcomes them shares in their wicked work.

Reflection

If you have a pound coin in your pocket, it could be worthless. According to the Royal Mint, there are millions of fakes in circulation, but how are we to know if we have one of them? As with anything else that attracts the attentions of forgers, the starting point for spotting the counterfeit is always an intimate familiarity with the genuine.

John feared for the infant churches under his pastoral charge. Young believers were susceptible in ways never seen before or since. The remaining eyewitnesses to Jesus' earthly ministry were few. With the Bible yet to be compiled and codified, the scriptures in circulation were like the coins in our pockets – a mixture of bona fide and bogus.

Desperate times require desperate measures, but surely the same apostle who has been exhorting us to love one another cannot now be insisting on such fierce intolerance? Did not Jesus himself make it clear that the wheat and the weeds must be allowed to grow up side by side (Matthew 13:24–30)? Surely ours is not to judge.

John is not commending small-minded intolerance of anyone with values and beliefs contrary to our own. Any growing church will have its share of heresy! We each have to 'grow up' in faith (Ephesians 4:15), which inevitably means that a vibrant Christian fellowship will include people at various stages of development. John, however, refers here to 'deceivers': teachers who deny the basic truths of the gospel, especially the identity of Jesus Christ as the Word made flesh (John 1:14).

**As we become more acquainted with the genuine,
the fake will be revealed.**

STEVE AISTHORPE

Walk the talk

3 John 1–4 (NIV)

The elder, To my dear friend Gaius, whom I love in the truth.
Dear friend, I pray that you may enjoy good health and that
all may go well with you, even as your soul is getting along
well. It gave me great joy when some believers came and
testified to your faithfulness to the truth, telling how you
continue to walk in it. I have no greater joy than to hear that
my children are walking in the truth.

Reflection

The evidence we have from the first century shows that Gaius
was one of the most popular names in the Roman empire at
the time. We should not assume, therefore, that the
addressee of John's letter was any of the other men of that
name we find elsewhere in the New Testament. Gaius' name
was well chosen, however, as its root is the word for 'happiness' and, as news of Gaius reached John through the Christian grapevine, it filled him with 'great joy' (v. 3).

John's joy stemmed from hearing eyewitness reports that
the transforming power of the 'Spirit of truth' (a common
term for the Holy Spirit in John's gospel and letters) was bearing fruit in the life of his 'dear friend' (vv. 1–2, 11). Of course,
John's sources had not literally seen the invisible, inner

makeover that was going on, but they knew that his soul was 'getting along well' (v. 2) because they could observe its out-working. Gaius is reported to 'walk in the truth' (v. 4). In the New Testament, the term 'walking' is often used for the practical living out of faith.

Gaius had evidently allowed Christian truth to shape his character and direct his actions. He epitomised the term 'integrity', which literally means 'undivided'. The faith he professed and the lifestyle he practised were in harmony; there was no discord between belief and behaviour. No doubt his unified and wholehearted life not only brought joy to the apostle but was also a compelling witness to the not-yet-Christian people of his community and an inspiration to fellow believers.

**Lord, please grow more of your character in me –
and may all I think, do and say reflect that
inner change. Amen**

STEVE AISTHORPE

The love of strangers

3 John 5–8 (NIV)

Dear friend, you are faithful in what you are doing for the brothers and sisters, even though they are strangers to you. They have told the church about your love. You will do well to send them on their way in a manner that honours God. It was for the sake of the Name that they went out, receiving no help from the pagans. We ought therefore to show hospitality to such people so that we may work together for the truth.

Reflection

The term 'hospitality industry' says it all. In our own culture we have largely professionalised hospitality – trained staff extend a welcome for a price and guests expect nothing less than the service they pay for.

When John was writing, however, hospitality was a sacred duty as itinerant teachers were a crucial part of the fledgling church. A minority were frauds and John was adamant that there should be no welcome for them (2 John 7–11), but, while John was eager for the believers to avoid being hoodwinked by freeloaders, he longed for them to embrace the considerable blessings of genuine hospitality.

The word 'hospitality' in today's passage literally means 'love of strangers'. The New Testament reserves some of its warmest commendation for those who were exemplary in their hospitality – and some of its sternest condemnation for those who refused to be 'lovers of strangers'. Christian leaders are to be lovers of hospitality (Titus 1:8). Followers of Jesus Christ are to 'be eager to practise hospitality' (Romans 12:13, NLT). The earliest commentary on Romans captured the proactive sense of it perfectly and is a prophetic word to a culture that has institutionalised hospitality and encouraged fear of strangers: 'We are not just to receive the stranger when he comes to us, but actually to enquire often, look carefully, for strangers, to pursue them and search them out' (Origen, c. 185–254).

John received accounts of Gaius' lifestyle and could tell that he was walking in the truth because his open heart had led to an open home and an open hand (vv. 5–8).

'Do not forget to entertain strangers,
for by so doing some people have entertained angels
without knowing it' (Hebrews 13:2).

STEVE AISTHORPE

Diotrephes: an example to avoid

3 John 9–11 (NIV)

I wrote to the church, but Diotrephes, who loves to be first, will not welcome us. So when I come, I will call attention to what he is doing, spreading malicious nonsense about us. Not satisfied with that, he even refuses to welcome other believers. He also stops those who want to do so and puts them out of the church. Dear friend, do not imitate what is evil but what is good. Anyone who does what is good is from God. Anyone who does what is evil has not seen God.

Reflection

Those in positions of authority tend to get a bad press. It seems that Lord Acton's oft-quoted observation that 'power tends to corrupt and absolute power corrupts absolutely' (1887) does indeed have a basis in truth.

Diotrephes' rejection of legitimate authority (v. 9), his malicious gossip and determination that others should follow his unloving example (v. 10) all stem from a desire 'to be first' (v. 9). It is no secret that pride and vanity lie at the root of most conflicts in local churches.

John would remember his own quest for power, the indignant response of his fellow disciples and the gentle rebuke of Jesus as he explained the radically alternative dynamics of leadership in his upside-down kingdom (Mark 10:35–45). He had no intention, however, of allowing the Diotrephes situation to fester. As we shall see tomorrow, rather than hide behind pen and ink, he plans to tackle the matter face to face in the near future (3 John 13–14). Despite being unrestrained in his unmasking of Diotrephes, he refused to enter into an arm's length war of words.

We all face the temptation to denigrate others for the sake of self-aggrandisement. It need not be blatant – just a subtle putting down or a slight exaggeration in our own favour. Jesus, who 'did not come to be served, but to serve' (Matthew 20:28), leads us into another way.

Jesus Christ, may you have supremacy in my life and your church. Amen

STEVE AISTHORPE

Demetrius: an example to follow

3 John 12–14 (NIV)

Demetrius is well spoken of by everyone – and even by the truth itself. We also speak well of him, and you know that our testimony is true. I have much to write you, but I do not want to do so with pen and ink. I hope to see you soon, and we will talk face to face. Peace to you. The friends here send their greetings. Greet the friends there by name.

Reflection

During a quiet day, the retreat leader set me the task of prayerfully reviewing my life and expressing it as a map, noting the major junctions and what had happened there to take me in one direction rather than another. As I reviewed the map that emerged, I noted that, at each crossroads, there had been a significant person. In some cases, they were people with whom I had an ongoing relationship. In other cases, it seemed that God had brought them across my path for a particular reason or even at a specific moment.

Occasionally, such people challenged or even rebuked me. Often they encouraged me. On the whole, though, their influence was unconscious on their part. They each inspired me or confronted me not in their words but in their character, life and example. 'Mentors' have become fashionable in many contexts. The media expects high-profile personalities to be 'role models'. A recent survey found that young people frequently choose role models from celebrity culture. We all need role models, but must choose them wisely.

Demetrius was an outstanding role model. Not only did John appreciate him but he was also 'well spoken of by everyone' and endorsed by the 'truth itself' (v. 12). The presence of Christ in his life was self-evident. Here was a man to learn from and be inspired by, someone with qualities to emulate. Jesus alone should be the ultimate focus of our attention (Hebrews 12:2) and the only yardstick for comparison (Ephesians 4:13). In his providence, however, God provides both role models and, amazingly and usually without our awareness, uses us to inspire, encourage and challenge others.

Loving Father, thank you for each person you have used, and are using, to direct my path and shape my character. Amen

STEVE AISTHORPE

Week 2: Group study questions

Demetrius: an example to follow
(14 December)

1 Share examples of people you feel have had a positive influence in your life, and explain why that is.

2 What character traits did they demonstrate? Which would you particularly like to cultivate?

3 'We all need role models, but must choose them wisely.' How can you be proactive in identifying mentors or positive influences for the next stage of your spiritual journey?

4 How can we build fellowship and support within this group, and within our church community?

5 How can you 'be Demetrius' to others in your families, workplaces and neighbourhoods?

Light in the darkness

AMY BOUCHER PYE

A Saviour for all

Matthew 1:1–6 (TNIV)

This is the genealogy of Jesus the Messiah the son of David, the son of Abraham: Abraham was the father of Isaac, Isaac the father of Jacob, Jacob the father of Judah and his brothers, Judah the father of Perez and Zerah, whose mother was Tamar, Perez the father of Hezron, Hezron the father of Ram, Ram the father of Amminadab, Amminadab the father of Nahshon, Nahshon the father of Salmon, Salmon the father of Boaz, whose mother was Rahab, Boaz the father of Obed, whose mother was Ruth, Obed the father of Jesse, and Jesse the father of King David. David was the father of Solomon, whose mother had been Uriah's wife.

Reflection

Did your eyes glaze over as you read this genealogy? So often when reading the Bible we skip over these unfamiliar names. Amminadab? Nahshon? Who are they to me?

There are treasures buried in this list, though, that the original readers would have understood. For instance, unlike most ancient genealogists, Matthew includes women: as well as Mary, Jesus' mother, he names Tamar, Rahab, Ruth and Bathsheba (Uriah's wife). He also includes outcasts (Rahab was a Gentile prostitute), those wronged by men (Tamar had to trick her father-in-law so that he would fulfil his legal obligation for her to marry his son) and those of the 'wrong religion' (as a Moabite, Ruth would have been excluded from the synagogue).

With this, Matthew implies that, although Jesus comes from royal stock (via King David), his roots and very DNA are in those who are marginalised and wronged. As Messiah, he was anointed to save those high in society – and those who were not. Including these so-called questionable women may also be Matthew's way of preparing his readers for the unusual circumstances of Jesus' birth, including that he was born to an unmarried woman.

The way Jesus comes to earth blows apart our preconceptions of how the king of the world should make himself known to his people. He may be high and mighty, but he is also lowly and humble.

**Lord Jesus Christ, as we prepare to celebrate
your coming, open our eyes to those
at the margins of society.**

AMY BOUCHER PYE

Divine passive

Matthew 1:15–16 (TNIV)

Matthan [was] the father of Jacob, and Jacob the father of Joseph, the husband of Mary, and Mary was the mother of Jesus who is called the Messiah.

Reflection

What a difference a bit of grammar can make (so says Michael J. Wilkins in *The NIV Application Commentary: Matthew*, Zondervan, 2004). Throughout the genealogy, Matthew has used the Greek verb *gennao* in the active voice, such as 'Abraham fathered Isaac.' After 40 instances of the active verb, he turns here to the passive when describing Mary and Jesus – in the NIV, Joseph was the husband of Mary, 'of whom was born Jesus'. Matthew's readers would have noticed this shift, for it implies what many grammarians 'call a "divine passive", where God is the assumed agent of the action' (p. 63).

In editing classes, our teachers drummed it into us always to use the active voice, but sometimes, as we see here, the passive is quite simply divine. In a simple shift of language, Matthew points to God at work. Watch out, he says, for what comes next is something new and completely different.

When it comes to his people, God is always the divine initiator. Mary responded to him saying yes to God working literally in her body: 'What is conceived in her is from the Holy Spirit' (v. 20). Luke's gospel records her humble and willing response when the angel announced that she would conceive a child through the 'power of the Most High' (Luke 1:35): 'I am the Lord's servant… may it be to me according to your word' (v. 38). Mary's receptivity changed the world.

How does God want to break through to us today? He may not want us to change the world, but, rather, parts of our world. Perhaps he is opening a new opportunity for service or inviting us to mentor someone or prompting us to extinguish anger and repair a broken relationship. Whatever it is, as we are still and listen for his voice, we will hear his words of love and guidance. May we be as Mary was that day, responding with open hands and a receptive heart.

**The angel Gabriel said to Mary,
'For no word from God will ever fail' (Luke 1:37).**

AMY BOUCHER PYE

When plans change

Matthew 1:18–19 (TNIV)

This is how the birth of Jesus the Messiah came about: his mother Mary was pledged to be married to Joseph, but before they came together, she was found to be pregnant through the Holy Spirit. Because Joseph her husband was a righteous man and did not want to expose her to public disgrace, he had in mind to divorce her quietly.

Reflection

The betrothal had taken place and Mary and Joseph were pledged to one another in marriage. Things didn't turn out as they had planned, however, as, before they 'came together' (Matthew's delicate way of implying that they had not had sexual relations), Joseph learned that Mary was expecting a child. At that time, she was probably four months' pregnant, having spent time with her relative Elizabeth, who herself was expecting her son John the Baptist (as we learn in Luke's account).

Courting and marriage were different in biblical times from how they are now. Back then, young men and women would be betrothed to each other for about a year before they entered into marriage. The betrothal would involve exchanging gifts and signing a prenuptial agreement, which gave the man rights over the woman. To break those legal ties entailed divorce. That, then, is what Joseph faced.

Imagine what Joseph was feeling – shocked, angry, hurt, disappointed, indignant, deflated. His plans for spending his life with Mary were shattered. In an instant, everything changed. What was he to do? He could marry her, but that would condone her sin of adultery, leaving him impure before God. He could demand a public divorce, but that would humiliate her publicly and perhaps even result in her death by stoning. He settled on a third option, a private divorce, which would ensure his holiness before God while safeguarding her life.

Your day may be filled with preparations for the feast of Christmas. Stop for a moment, however, to put yourself in Joseph's shoes and forget what comes next in the story. With Joseph, every cell in his body cries out in anguish, 'Why? Why did she? Why me? Why, God? Oh, why?'

'As the heavens are higher than the earth,
so are my ways higher than your ways and my thoughts
than your thoughts' (Isaiah 55:9).

AMY BOUCHER PYE

The son of David

Matthew 1:20–21 (TNIV)

But after he had considered this, an angel of the Lord appeared to him in a dream and said, 'Joseph son of David, do not be afraid to take Mary home as your wife, because what is conceived in her is from the Holy Spirit. She will give birth to a son, and you are to give him the name Jesus, because he will save his people from their sins.'

Reflection

After Joseph learned that Mary was pregnant, he despaired about the future. No doubt she told him about the child's divine origins, but how could he believe her? Such a story was inconceivable. So, as we saw yesterday, Joseph chose the best of the unwelcome options – divorce. God, however, had different plans.

Joseph awoke from his dream and instantly knew the truth of Mary's pregnancy. The night before, his hopes for marriage had been shattered, but, in the light of day, he could see a whole new reality shaping up, including him being the legal father of one who was to become the Saviour of his people. Surely Joseph woke up a changed man, no longer despairing but embracing a new life.

When the angel called Joseph 'son of David', it was to establish Jesus' divine lineage. (Incidentally, Joseph is the only one to be called a son of David in the New Testament other than Jesus himself.) That is also why the angel instructed Joseph to name Jesus, for that entailed him formally acknowledging Jesus as his son and, thus, a son of David. Joseph may not have been the biological father of Jesus, but his role as his earthly father was vital.

God speaking to his children hasn't changed since biblical times – he still breaks through, whether in a dream, an insight gleaned from the Bible, wisdom from friends, our time of prayer or other means. How is God reaching out to you on this busy day, when you might be finishing up work or school, buying last-minute presents, preparing food, reading Christmas missives or generally being stressed out? As you go forth, know that God will speak, even in the midst of all of this.

Father, I am busy with many things.
Help me to choose what is best.

AMY BOUCHER PYE

The virgin will conceive

Matthew 1:22–23 (TNIV)

All this took place to fulfil what the Lord had said through the prophet: 'The virgin will conceive and give birth to a son…'

Reflection

Matthew's concise account highlights the miracle of the virgin birth, which was foretold by the prophet Isaiah (7:14). God, through his Holy Spirit, overshadowed Mary and conceived in her Jesus, who is both divine and human. It's a mind-boggling concept of the Trinity at work: God, the creator of the universe, descends through his Holy Spirit to his creation in the person of Jesus, one who is God yet man and, thus, one of the created. Being divine, Jesus can fulfil the meaning of his given name, 'Yahweh saves'. Being human, Jesus can relate to us completely. The whole thing is utterly brilliant.

God didn't stop there, though, for, following Jesus' birth, death and resurrection, there was then Pentecost, when he poured out his Holy Spirit on his people. As the Holy Spirit overshadowed Mary and thus brought about the indwelling of Jesus, we too can host Jesus. Not physically, of course, but Christ living in us transforms us, cleansing us and bringing forth the gifts and fruit of the Spirit (including wisdom, under-standing, knowledge, right judgement and love, joy, peace, gentleness, faith and self-control). What better gifts this Christmas season?

Jesus dwelling in us, which is made possible by the incarnation, is echoed in scripture. Jesus referred to it at various times, such as when instructing his disciples before he died ('I am in my Father, and you are in me, and I am in you', John 14:20) or his final prayer for them ('I in them and you in me', John 17:23). The apostle Paul reflected this new reality in his letters, such as 'Christ in you, the hope of glory' (Colossians 1:27) or 'I have been crucified with Christ and I no longer live, but Christ lives in me' (Galatians 2:20).

Celebrating the incarnation is a wonderful opportunity to reflect on the reality of Jesus dwelling in us and rejoice.

'I pray that out of his glorious riches he may strengthen you with power through his Spirit in your inner being, so that Christ may dwell in your hearts through faith' (Ephesians 3:16–17).

AMY BOUCHER PYE

Messiah, Immanuel, Jesus

Matthew 1:23–25 (TNIV)

'And they will call him Immanuel' (which means 'God with us'). When Joseph woke up, he did what the angel of the Lord had commanded him and took Mary home as his wife. But he had no union with her until she gave birth to a son. And he gave him the name Jesus.

Reflection

While Luke's account focuses on Mary and her response to God's work, Matthew recounts Joseph's willingness to follow God's plans. Joseph was obedient immediately: he fulfilled the second part of the betrothal, which was the official marriage ceremony, and he named his son Jesus, as instructed by the angel.

What's in a name? In biblical times, a name would often connote characteristics that the parents believed the child would embody. Along these lines, God, through his angel, told Joseph to name his son Jesus, which means (as mentioned earlier) 'Yahweh saves' and what Jesus saves his people from is their sins. I don't think Joseph had any idea of how Jesus would do this, but he welcomed it from a distance.

Matthew's account also gives Jesus two other names or titles – Messiah and Immanuel. 'Messiah' is the Hebrew word for one anointed for a specific task (with 'Christ' being the Greek rendering of this word). Matthew used this term to signal to his Jewish audience that this was the coming Saviour, for whom they had been waiting for generations to bring about God's promised deliverance.

Finally, 'Immanuel' means 'God with us' – God himself took human form in Jesus. God is with us because Jesus saves us from our sins, for sin is what separates us from God. Once Jesus rescues us from this fallen state, we enjoy Immanuel, God with us.

Jesus the anointed one; Jesus who saves; Jesus, God with us. What's in a name? Simply, it is the whole gospel message.

Lord Jesus, you are the anointed one, the God who lives with us, the one who saves. As we praise and worship you this day, fill us with your presence and love. Help us to reach out to a world aching to hear your message of good news.

AMY BOUCHER PYE

The death of innocence

Matthew 2:13, 16 (TNIV)

An angel of the Lord appeared to Joseph in a dream. 'Get up,' he said, 'take the child and his mother and escape to Egypt. Stay there until I tell you, for Herod is going to search for the child to kill him.'... When Herod realised that he had been outwitted by the Magi, he was furious, and he gave orders to kill all the boys in Bethlehem and its vicinity who were two years old and under.

Reflection

Today, we return to the story of Jesus' birth and meet Herod, a jealous, volatile and violent king. Hearing about the new king of the Jews, he wanted to eradicate any potential competition, so, when he realised that the magi were not returning to tell him where Jesus was living as planned, he decided to kill all the little boys in Bethlehem who were two and under. Satisfied, he thought his kingship was secure.

This massacre of around 30 boys (for Bethlehem was a small village) wasn't outside of Herod's character. As Michael Green says in *The Message of Matthew* (IVP, 1988, pp. 70–71), Herod had his wife and her mother killed as well as three of his sons and, when he was dying, he ordered that all the notable men of Jerusalem be killed in the hippodrome.

Herod may have been a powerful king, but his plans to eliminate Jesus were foiled for Joseph was warned in a dream and he obeyed the angel's direction, trekking into safe territory in Egypt. Clearly our heavenly king was not limited by the wickedness of earthly kings.

Why, though, did those little boys have to die? Why did all those mothers have to weep for their slain children? We just don't know, for it is wrapped up in the fall of humanity and the problem of evil, but we can be certain about God's promises that he will comfort the comfortless and bring hope to the hopeless. We know that he too grieves the loss of children who were so young.

Heavenly Father, we don't understand why you sometimes allow innocent people to die. Strengthen our faith and help us to know more of your character.

AMY BOUCHER PYE

Week 3: Group study questions

A Saviour for all (15 December)

1 In pairs or small groups, take one or two characters from the list in this passage and briefly share what you know about them. Look up (either now or later) any with whom you're not familiar.

2 Why do you think the women were included when that wasn't common practice at the time of writing?

3 'Genealogy' (verse 1) is the Greek word for 'genesis'. In what ways is the gospel of Matthew a book of beginnings like the book of Genesis?

4 Why is it so important for Matthew to emphasise that Jesus is descended from Abraham and David, given the audience he's writing for? What do people we know need to understand about Jesus?

5 As individuals or as a group, think of one way in which you can make Jesus known to others this Christmas.

Word incarnate: John 1:1–16

ANDY JOHN

In the beginning

John 1:1–2 (NRSV)

In the beginning was the Word, and the Word was with God, and the Word was God. He was in the beginning with God.

Reflection

I can remember going to a visitor centre that had an interactive exhibition about the history of the Celtic people. There was a video presentation that lasted about ten minutes – a heady concoction of stories of tribal warfare and inter-clan rivalries. We were given a whistle-stop tour of the last 2,000 years of Celtic history and were told we had to peer back through the mists of time and understand who we were then in order to understand who we are now.

At the beginning of John's gospel, too, we are invited to look back as far as we can in order to do much the same. We cannot understand what God is doing now without looking back to the 'beginning'.

John's gospel is different from the other gospels in many ways and its opening verses are unique. There is no account of the birth of Jesus or history of God's dealings with his people. Instead, we start at the start – a bit like Genesis – and what we find there is 'the Word'.

John is likely to have had several ideas about what he meant when he used this phrase, but the most obvious meaning is actually quite simple: that, from the very beginning, God has spoken and revealed himself, and this 'Word' has a real connection with God. He is the same as God, sharing eternity, sharing identity and sharing purpose.

This means that the whole book must be read and understood in that light. The Galilean would be no magician, no soothsayer. He would not be another prophet in a long line of holy people. He is nothing less than God, speaking God's words, doing God's works, and he has plans for the world, for you and for me.

Gracious God, your Word is from all eternity. You have revealed yourself to all people and shown yourself as Lord Almighty. Speak again, so I may hear afresh what things both great and small you wish me to hear. Amen

ANDY JOHN

The light of all people

John 1:3–4 (NRSV)

All things came into being through him, and without him not one thing came into being. What has come into being in him was life and the life was the light of all people.

Reflection

Some of us may recall the undignified role we were sometimes given at school of being a 'gopher'. There were no mobiles or online messenger services in those days! Our task was to carry a note from one class and teacher to another, and that was the extent of our responsibility. There was nothing great or creative about it; we were the passive bearers of another's words.

In the few words that make up today's passage, however, John seeks to draw out the meaning of the idea he has given us in his opening sentences. He does this by using the idea of an agent – that is, someone who acts on another's behalf. He is not merely the bearer of news or a message as we were, though, but the active agent, bringing into being the things God wishes.

The meaning is clear: God's full and unimpeded Lordship over all creation is revealed through his Word. 'Not one thing' are the words John uses to emphasise the full extent of his sovereign reign. If God is seen to be sovereign by the work of his Word, then he can have no equals. If the reign of God is fully revealed by his actions, then he has no peers and no competitors.

It is only implicit at this stage, but we can see two themes emerging: the greatness of Jesus and the possibility of a relationship with God through him. We will find John drawing out both themes as we work through this chapter, but, for now, let us hold the weight of these extraordinary truths in our mind's eye. This is the true greatness of God, who is worthy of endless praise and adoration.

Lord of all creation, you sustain in being all that is and none can compare with you. As you spoke and brought life into existence, speak into the smallness of our own lives so that something of your greatness may be known and worshipped, through Jesus Christ our Lord. Amen

ANDY JOHN

Not understood, not overcome

John 1:5 (NASB)

The light shines in the darkness and the darkness did not comprehend it [or '… did not overcome it', NRSV].

Reflection

John has told us that the source of all life is God's Word, by whose power everything has come into being, and this life is the very essence of what makes people unique: 'The life was the light of all people', he says (v. 4). Now he draws this line of thought to a close by using a clever word that can mean two things – and he probably intends us to understand it as having both meanings.

The first meaning is that of 'understood'. The darkness (by which John means all that is not God) has not 'understood' the light because light and darkness are opposites and mutually excluding. The darkness cannot perceive or make sense of something so utterly alien to it that they remain apart.

The second meaning is that of 'overcome' (or, as the GNT has it, 'the darkness has never put it out'). The meaning here is that of power or enduring force. The darkness cannot overwhelm the light because the light will always pierce the gloom. To put it another way, darkness cannot remain dark when it is touched by the rays of light.

In both of these meanings, John intends us to see the enduring strength and might of Christ. The reality of God's apparent absence might seem overwhelming, but light still invades the darkness and transforms it.

Across the years, I have encountered people who find this truth to be personally important. Patients in hospital, those facing awful crises or uncertainty, damaged lives that appear to be impervious to hope suddenly discover the light piercing their own darkness. This is not in any way to diminish their challenges, but, rather, to set out the hope we have in God. The gospel of Christ means that lives and hopeless situations can be transformed.

Come, gentle Saviour and light of the world.
Shine light into hidden places long absent from
your love, and let that light settle, heal and restore
your own good image in us. Amen

ANDY JOHN

Made through him

John 1:10–11 (NRSV)

He was in the world, and the world came into being through him; yet the world did not know him. He came to what was his own and his own people did not accept him.

Reflection

On this Christmas Day, I wish you a merry Christmas and that Jesus will fill you with the joy of his birth and the wonder of his coming. Today, let's pray for 'all those who know not the Lord Jesus, or who love him not, or who by sin have grieved his heart of love' (words from the traditional service of lessons and carols). I find these words deeply moving because they convey some of the heartache in God for his creation.

In today's passage, we hear similar words, and they too convey a kind of pain. The gospel writer continues by moving from the person called to proclaim God to the nation called to do the same. Here, the fourth gospel sits closely with the others in terms of the way in which Jesus is announced as Israel's Saviour, and the force of these words comes from the way in which Jesus is rejected. The book of Isaiah contains the famous words, familiar perhaps from Handel's great work, *Messiah*, that God's servant was 'despised and rejected by men; a man of sorrows, and acquainted with grief; and as one from whom men hide their faces he was despised, and we esteemed him not' (Isaiah 53:3, ESV).

There are many reasons Jesus is rejected today. Some people believe that faith is ridiculous, others do not see how Jesus is relevant to them and still others consider his call so all-embracing that it is too much to bear. While it is not really any kind of comfort, knowing that the rejection of Jesus has a wider context and history and being aware of this bigger picture may help us when he is still rejected today. Although it will not always be so (Philippians 2:10–11), somehow in the mystery of God the rejection of Jesus, witnessed in his life and death, continues and the world still does 'not know him' (v. 10).

You are the Saviour of the world, Lord Jesus Christ, born to save us from our sins, showing us the Father's glory. All praise to you on this and every day. Amen

ANDY JOHN

Children of God

John 1:12–13 (NRSV)

But to all who received him, who believed in his name, he gave power to become children of God, who were born, not of blood or of the will of the flesh or of the will of man, but of God.

Reflection

In today's passage John lays out the glorious truth of our salvation, which is God's doing and not our own. At first sight it might seem strange to list obvious but irrelevant sources for such a thing – born 'not of blood or of the will of flesh' (v. 13) – but John has an important point in mind. It is that grace is transmitted by neither race nor inheritance, nor by any other human means, but is the free gift of God (Ephesians 2:8).

The image of being reborn or born again will be used powerfully a little later in this gospel (John 3). It describes an act so instrumental in defining who we are and so transforming in its effects that nothing less than a picture of new life and birth will suffice. Christians have not always agreed on how this happens, and it is sad that such an extraordinary image has become a divisive issue. Given the significance of the phrase, it cannot be true that there are born-again Christians and not-born-again Christians. To belong to Christ, we must all be born again. If we are his, we are born again, irrespective of what others may say.

It is all made a little easier if we focus not on the 'when' or 'how' we came to Christ and received new birth, but, rather, on the fact that we have indeed received Christ and been born again. Christians who receive this free gift of grace and understand it as such are less likely to judge others. When we remember that the important matter for Christ is how such faith is living in us and producing the fruit of his grace, it restores this wonderful image to its rightful place.

Lord Jesus, we offer praise and honour to you,
for we are yours by grace and your gift of new birth.
May the fruit of your grace overflow in me for your
greater glory. Amen

ANDY JOHN

We have seen his glory

John 1:14 (NRSV)

And the Word became flesh and lived among us, and we have seen his glory, the glory as of a father's only son, full of grace and truth.

Reflection

Family photos can reveal a great deal. We see likenesses of children in their parents that are hard to quantify. Something of mum or dad lives in their offspring in the most uncanny way. This is a picture we might hold on to as we explore the extraordinary words in today's passage.

There are few Bible verses that have more weight than John 1:14. We are told how God's Word, the agent of his creation and means of relating to the world, became human. Yet, somehow, he retained his divine nature, reflecting God's own image and essence, full of grace and truth.

John brings several strands together in this verse. First, God stepped into human history when he 'became flesh and lived among us'. Second, the uniqueness of Jesus, the 'only son', is announced. Third, the 'incarnate God' (that is, God become human) remains fully God – bearing his likeness, reflecting his glory.

We can say that in this is the very essence of the gospel. Christians believe that Jesus' life and ministry, his teaching and miracles and his death and resurrection all make sense because he was no mere man. Jesus understands our every weakness (Hebrews 4:15), but, because he is God in nature, he is able to do a great deal about our weaknesses, our sins and our mortality. If this is true for individuals, it is true for all people and all history, too, because God is 'in the world' and not apart from it.

It is this that makes faith in Christ so compelling. God truly has come to us and, from within our humanity, redeems and saves us. The old saying retains its power still: the Son of God became the Son of Man so that the sons and daughters of man might become sons and daughters of God.

**Lord Jesus Christ, you know our every weakness
and we rejoice in your saving strength to win us.
Praise to you, Father, Son and Holy Spirit, one gracious
and holy God, world without end. Amen**

ANDY JOHN

Grace on grace

John 1:16 (NRSV)

From his fullness we have all received, grace upon grace.

Reflection

From where I lived as a child, it was possible to see much of the expanse of Cardigan Bay – a huge area encompassing most of the Irish Sea. On a good day, I could see the most southerly parts of Wales and also the Llyn Peninsula to the north, taking in Snowdon for good measure. It never ceased to leave me awestruck, so vast and great was the territory. I suspect people who work in fields such as astronomy or marine biology feel a bit like this as they contemplate the vastness of their subject matter.

In today's reading, I think John intends us to be struck by the scale of God's grace. The superlatives he uses press home the sheer wonder of God's goodness to his creation. First, from his 'fullness' we have 'all' received. In God's economy there are no half measures, only fullness. What God gives to his creation is nothing less than his very self and in his entirety. It is also to *all* his creation he gives, so that, potentially, no one is excluded from knowing Jesus' love. A little later in this gospel (in John 3) we will read how God loved the world so much that he gave his only Son for its salvation. The generosity of that truth is anticipated here.

Second, this vast and generous gift is endless; it is a 'grace upon grace'. I have often wondered what these words mean and I am still a little unsure. Undoubtedly, God's blessings are always new and keep coming so that we may explore them for all time. I wonder if these words also anticipate the coming of the Holy Spirit, because the Spirit is the one whose work among us continues each day. If this is correct, we have, again, early seeds of the Trinity here: God the Father sending the Son, Christ, to live among us, and the Spirit anticipated as the means by which lives are renewed in grace.

Gracious God, may we all today receive the grace you have promised from the fullness that is yours, and may we rejoice in the wonder of your goodness. Amen

ANDY JOHN

Week 4: Group study questions

Grace on grace (28 December)

1 Read John 1:1–16 together, and then share particular verses that caught your attention as you read or listened.

2 As we consider 'the sheer wonder of God's goodness to his creation', we confess that we ourselves have not been good to God's creation. How can you show love to and care for our world – its birds, animals, resources?

3 Reflect in silence, or with quiet music playing, on what 'grace on grace' might mean for you over Christmas and in the year ahead.

4 How might God be asking us to 'testify concerning that light'?

5 Pray for friends, family or others you know to experience the fullness of God's grace.

Psalms of hope

MARGARET CUNDIFF

Choose your way with care

Psalm 1:1–3 (NRSV)

Happy are those who do not follow the advice of the wicked, or take the path that sinners tread, or sit in the seat of scoffers; but their delight is in the law of the Lord, and on his law they meditate day and night. They are like trees planted by streams of water, which yield their fruit in its season, and their leaves do not wither. In all that they do, they prosper.

Reflection

It is so easy to accept bad advice. Somehow it is always so attractive, so plausible, with its 'you know it makes sense' overtones. 'Beware,' says the psalmist. 'Learn the lesson of true happiness which is to be found in studying and obeying the law of the Lord.' 'The law' perhaps conjures up for us dry and dusty tomes of legal rules, regulations and restrictions, shot through with dire warnings of penalty clauses. But the law of the Lord refers to the first five books of the Bible, the wonderful history of God's dealings with his people, of his love and guiding hand, enabling them to live out their lives.

The Hebrew word for 'law', *Torah*, means guidance, or instruction, on how to enjoy the full life God intends for all of us. Surely it's worth giving it our full attention. Then we shall draw strength and insight, gain vision and purpose, and become the people God intended we should be, fruitful in service for him and for our fellow men and women.

The analogy of the fruitful healthy tree and the person who delights in knowing and obeying God's word brings home the joy and value of God's word for us each day. We draw from the water of life our nourishment, our strength. We are enabled to grow and develop; to stand tall and straight; to provide sustenance for others, so that they too might know and grow; to be 'something beautiful' (and useful) for God and to be truly happy, 'blessed' in our daily lives.

'Thus says the Lord: Stand at the crossroads, and look, and ask for the ancient paths, where the good way lies; and walk in it, and find rest for your souls. But they said, "We will not walk in it"' (Jeremiah 6:16).

Lord, help me to choose the right way, to listen to your voice, to grow in understanding, to be fruitful in service and to praise your name every day of my life.

MARGARET CUNDIFF

Creator and sustainer

Psalm 8:3–9 (NRSV)

When I look at your heavens, the work of your fingers, the moon and the stars that you have established; what are human beings that you are mindful of them, mortals that you care for them? Yet you have made them a little lower than God, and crowned them with glory and honour. You have given them dominion over the works of your hands; you have put all things under their feet, all sheep and oxen, and also the beasts of the field, the birds of the air, and the fish of the sea, whatever passes along the paths of the seas. O Lord, our Sovereign, how majestic is your name in all the earth!

Reflection

On the last night of our 'winter sun' holiday in Tenerife, I stood on our balcony looking up into the sky, the bright moon shining over the sea, the stars like jewels, the air like wine. The following night I stood in our garden in North Yorkshire, well wrapped up on that cold frosty evening, and looked up into the sky again. The same moon, stars and brilliant clear sky, and I marvelled at the glorious majestic creation of God, the world he has made and given us to enjoy and share. I found myself singing a children's chorus: 'There are hundreds and thousands and millions of planets, but God knows every one, and God knows me!'

The psalmist in his time sang a hymn of praise to God for the gift of creation, realising how tiny and insignificant he was in relation to it all, yet recognising that awesomeness of being a steward of creation, in relationship with the creator God. He speaks of 'our Sovereign', the one worshipped and praised in heaven, as Isaiah saw in his vision of seraphs around the throne who cried, 'Holy, holy, holy is the Lord of hosts; the whole earth is full of his glory' (Isaiah 6:3). Yet he is also the one who reaches down from heaven to earth to enable humanity to know him, to love him and to tend the creatures of land, sea and sky.

Creator of the universe, watch over us and keep us in the light of your presence. May our praise continually blend with that of all creation, until we come together to the eternal joys which you promise in your love, through Jesus Christ our Lord. Amen.

MARGARET CUNDIFF

How long, O Lord?

Psalm 13 (NRSV)

How long, O Lord? Will you forget me for ever? How long will you hide your face from me? How long must I bear pain in my soul, and have sorrow in my heart all day long? How long shall my enemy be exalted over me? Consider and answer me, O Lord my God! Give light to my eyes, or I will sleep the sleep of death, and my enemy will say, 'I have prevailed'; my foes will rejoice because I am shaken. But I trusted in your steadfast love; my heart shall rejoice in your salvation. I will sing to the Lord, because he has dealt bountifully with me.

Reflection

In the NRSV this psalm is headed 'Prayer for deliverance from enemies'. The enemy referred to may have been an opposing power waging war, physical illness, depression or the fear of death – that 'last enemy' that Paul writes about in his first letter to the Corinthians ('The last enemy to be destroyed is death', 1 Corinthians 15:26). Whoever or whatever the enemy was, the psalmist felt ignored, forgotten by God, isolated, alone, almost to the point of being totally overwhelmed. The God who he knew loved him had somehow turned away from him, for there was no answer to his prayer for help, and he was sinking into the depths from which there would be no escape. He could almost hear his enemy celebrating the victory over him, and still no help came. The love he had trusted in was steadfast, he knew that; but it was in the past, so what about now? But the reminder of that steadfast love gave him hope for the future, in spite of how it seemed, and he knew within himself that he would again rejoice, sing for joy and praise the Lord for bringing him through his trouble.

There are times in our lives when perhaps we too cry, 'How long, O Lord, how long?' God seems distant, even uncaring, and yet we know he cannot and will not forsake us, even though the circumstances we find ourselves in seem to deny it. Jesus himself went through that, but he came through to know again the joy of the steadfast love of his Father which had always been there, and which would bring him – and us – through to victory.

**This New Year's Eve, thanks be to God,
who gives us the victory through our Lord Jesus Christ
(1 Corinthians 15:57).**

MARGARET CUNDIFF

Look up and see the glory of God

Psalm 19:1–6 (NRSV)

The heavens are telling the glory of God; and the firmament proclaims his handiwork. Day to day pours forth speech, and night to night declares knowledge. There is no speech, nor are there words; their voice is not heard; yet their voice goes out through all the earth, and their words to the end of the world. In the heavens he has set a tent for the sun, which comes out like a bridegroom from his wedding canopy, and like a strong man runs its course with joy. Its rising is from the end of the heavens, and its circuit to the end of them; and nothing is hidden from its heat.

Reflection

In the symphony orchestra of the sky, chorus and principals combine to make music to inspire and delight us. God himself is author, choreographer and conductor, and all we need to do is to look up and listen with our eyes, our hearts, our minds and our souls to the wordless, soundless music of heaven – the song of creation with its light and shade, its bursts of dramatic power and energy, the gentle harmony of the passage of time through to the whisper of a new dawn. The story is retold day by day; we are welcomed without charge to the performance, and nothing is spared that we might personally experience the almighty power and glory of God. There is no need for words – God's glory seen in the heavens transcends speech, and yet it spells out the story so that even a child can look, marvel and receive.

From the dawn of creation, men and women have gazed into the sky and marvelled at the glory of it all, sensing the existence of a power that has made and held it – a power so great that it must be God, for the glory could not have happened just by chance.

What marvellous pen-pictures we have here of the sun, likened to the bridegroom coming in his glory on his wedding day, and the proud runner striding out, enjoying his physical power. Here are beauty, excitement, glory and confidence to be seen, admired and enjoyed. As we read these verses, may we get a vision of the glory of God, written large in his heaven.

As we begin the New Year, remember that the glory of God is there for you to see and hear, if you will lift your eyes and heart to heaven.

MARGARET CUNDIFF

The cry of the heart

Psalm 22:1–5 (NRSV)

My God, my God, why have you forsaken me? Why are you so far from helping me, from the words of my groaning? O my God, I cry by day, but you do not answer; and by night, but find no rest. Yet you are holy, enthroned on the praises of Israel. In you our ancestors trusted; they trusted, and you delivered them. To you they cried, and were saved; in you they trusted, and were not put to shame.

Reflection

We cannot read this psalm without hearing Jesus crying out in agony on the cross, being engulfed in the darkness, deeper than that which covered the world during the time of his dying and death. He cries out in the words of a psalm that he would have known from childhood, words of his ancestor David.

These words may have described David's own feelings of desolation at some point in his life, or were words of prophecy concerning his descendant. In Acts, Luke speaks of David as a prophet foretelling the suffering, death and resurrection of the Messiah (Acts 2:25–35). They also echo the cry of the human heart today, the cry of those going through intense pain, calling out to the God they know is there, the God they trust, but who somehow seems to have deserted them.

This psalm can help, for while it begins with that cry 'Why?', it goes on to recall God's love and care even from before birth, remembering the sustaining power of God along the way and giving a sure hope for the future. The psalmist looks forward to praising God, testifying of his experience of salvation, with a glorious vision of all nations worshipping the God who answers and saves. He also sees the promise of salvation for all the generations yet unborn – including our own! What began with 'My God, why?' ends in assurance, confidence and praise.

We look forward in hope, too, to the day when there will be no need for questions, only songs of praise and thanksgiving. Until then, psalms like this one will enable us to realise that we are not alone. Even in our darkest hour, God is with us, will save us and will never let us go.

**Hold thou thy cross
before my closing eyes.
Shine through the gloom
and point me to the skies.
Heaven's morning breaks,
and earth's vain shadows flee,
in life, in death, O Lord,
abide with me.**
Henry Francis Lyte

MARGARET CUNDIFF

The good shepherd

Psalm 23 (NRSV)

The Lord is my shepherd, I shall not want. He makes me lie down in green pastures; he leads me beside still waters; he restores my soul. He leads me in right paths for his name's sake. Even though I walk through the darkest valley, I fear no evil; for you are with me; your rod and your staff – they comfort me. You prepare a table before me in the presence of my enemies; you anoint my head with oil; my cup over-flows. Surely goodness and mercy shall follow me all the days of my life, and I shall dwell in the house of the Lord my whole life long.

Reflection

David was a shepherd all his life, first of all caring for his father's sheep, then leading and caring for his nation as king. His experience in killing marauding wild animals who were attacking the sheep proved to be the perfect training for disposing of those who would attack Israel, and the account of his victory over Goliath is probably one of the best-known Bible stories.

David was a good shepherd: he loved his flocks, both sheep and people, and he would have given his life for them. But David, the shepherd king, also needed someone to care for him, to guide and protect him, rescue him from danger and provide for him. He knew that God himself was his shepherd, so that he was safe and secure for all time, and would be brought through all dangers and temptations to share the joys of his shepherd King in heaven. So in this psalm he describes the joy of the relationship he shares with God – the assurance and peace he knows through trust and obedience; the comfort of being guided and protected throughout his life; and the goodness and mercy of God who is his shepherd and friend, providing food and refreshment along the way and a shared home for eternity.

This psalm has brought comfort and strength to millions, given hope and peace and joy to those going through their own dark valleys, and the assurance of a welcome home when life is done. It is a very personal testimony, but one that opens the way for others to share in that personal relationship with God too.

Jesus said, 'I am the good shepherd.
The good shepherd lays down his life for his sheep.'
He said it and he did it, so that we might live.

MARGARET CUNDIFF

Thanksgiving for healing

Psalm 30:1–5 (NRSV)

I will extol you, O Lord, for you have drawn me up, and did not let my foes rejoice over me. O Lord my God, I cried to you for help, and you have healed me. O Lord, you brought up my soul from Sheol, restored me to life from among those gone down to the Pit. Sing praises to the Lord, O you his faithful ones, and give thanks to his holy name. For his anger is but for a moment; his favour is for a lifetime. Weeping may linger for the night, but joy comes with the morning.

Reflection

The words of this psalm dance and sing – you can feel the throb of excitement, relief and pure joy. The psalmist's prayer for healing had been answered, he had been brought back from what seemed certain death, and now he wants to share the good news and tell of the love and power of God. This is not only a psalm of thanksgiving for one very special answer to prayer but a recognition of the loving purposes of God in every situation, even in those that seem so hard, so hopeless.

Suffering is real, tears flow, hearts come to breaking point, but just as night ends and morning comes, so light will return to our life. God will lift us out of death so we might dance for joy in his presence, testifying to his wonderful love for us, singing songs of praise to him.

The psalmist had also learned another very important lesson, one we do well to learn too. He had thought that when things were going well, nothing could move him, nothing could topple him – but he was wrong! It was only by the grace and love of God that he was preserved, not by his own strength and power. Trouble brought him to his senses, to admit his pride and to cry out for mercy (vv. 6–8).

Sometimes we need reminding that pride goes before a fall, but God will restore us and set us free in company with all those who also have discovered not only the rhythm of life, but the author of life. Then one day, as we enter into the glorious reality of eternity, what a party it will be, joining 'with angels and archangels, and all the company of heaven' in the presence of our Lord, forever.

Lord, give me the grace and the humility to see your hand in all things, and to sing your praise at all times.

MARGARET CUNDIFF

A sure hope

Psalm 33:16–22 (NRSV)

A king is not saved by his great army; a warrior is not delivered by his great strength. The war horse is a vain hope for victory, and by its great might it cannot save. Truly the eye of the Lord is on those who fear him, on those who hope in his steadfast love, to deliver their soul from death, and to keep them alive in famine. Our soul waits for the Lord; he is our help and shield. Our heart is glad in him, because we trust in his holy name. Let your steadfast love, O Lord, be upon us, even as we hope in you.

Reflection

This psalm is a hymn of praise to God who is creator, ruler, judge and saviour. The whole of the psalm should be read, so as to put into context our portion for today. It tells of our God who knows, watches and acts, and it tells of the futility of putting our trust in armies and weapons of war. But, in the words of the folk song, 'When will they ever learn, when will they ever learn?' – for 'they', read 'we' and 'I'.

The power struggles for supremacy go on between nations, groups and individuals. History is littered with terrible accounts of the suffering inflicted upon one another, and today it still continues. Wars, fighting, destruction, suffering, death. Winners rise and fall; victory is hollow, paid for in the currency of human misery.

Yet, thank God, there are always those who work for peace and understanding, who seek a better way – peacemakers and peacekeepers in 'the corridors of power'; aid organisations, and those who take out that aid and expertise to suffering people caught up in conflict; those who risk, and often give, their lives to get help to the needy, regardless of which side they are on. Such people are often unsung and unknown, but they are agents of God's love for all human beings.

Whose side is God on? Verses 18 and 19 may help us think that through.

And what about our response? Where is our ground for hope? Surely the power of love is our only hope, the steadfast love of the Lord, for it is the way of peace and victory, of freedom and life.

**O God, our help in ages past,
Our hope for years to come,
Be thou our guard while life shall last,
And our eternal home.**
Isaac Watts

MARGARET CUNDIFF

Firm on the rock

Psalm 40:1–3 (NRSV)

I waited patiently for the Lord; he inclined to me and heard my cry. He drew me up from the desolate pit, out of the miry bog, and set my feet upon a rock, making my steps secure. He put a new song in my mouth, a song of praise to our God. Many will see and fear, and put their trust in the Lord.

Reflection

A friend of mine once told me how, when he was a small boy in Ireland, he fell into a bog. He had the terrifying experience of being sucked down into the mud, until a boy, only a couple of years older than himself, heaved him up and out of it. He remembers then lying, filthy and frightened but safe, on firm ground again. He said, 'When I read Psalm 40, I relive it. I have been there – I know what it's like first-hand.'

When my colleague David and I were reading this psalm together, I recounted the story. 'Yes, Margaret,' he said, 'but our trouble is, we don't always realise we are stuck in the bog and need rescuing, do we?' I need to remember that, and I pass it on to you! Sometimes we fall into the miry bog of trouble and sin – often we jump in – but either way, we get stuck, and the more we struggle, the deeper we get. All we can do is to cry out to God, and wait. God does hear and answer, and will bring us to firm ground again, so that we might walk in his way on the right path. King David knew that through personal experience. He had everything to sing about: he had been rescued and restored; he was a walking, singing testimony. So we too can rejoice in what God has done for us – his saving power, restoration and renewal. We can share the good news with others, just as David does in this psalm.

But read on in the psalm from verse 12, where he writes of 'evils' and 'iniquities': it has happened again, and again… as it does in our lives. And yet the good news is that God keeps on reaching down, lifting us out of the mire, giving us another chance, setting us on the rock of his salvation. May we, like David, 'say continually, "Great is the Lord!"' (v. 16).

What did it cost God to stoop down and rescue me out of the mire? Read John 3:16.

MARGARET CUNDIFF

Week 5: Group study questions

A sure hope (5 January)

1   Read the whole of Psalm 33. Do you personally find it inspiring, or daunting in its positivity? How hopeful do you feel at the start of this new year?

2   What, or who, do you tend to put your trust in, if not God?

3   What does the psalmist say about honouring and fearing God together as a nation? What can we do as individuals/a small group/a church to encourage this?

4   Are there situations where you 'wait in hope for the Lord'? How can we support each other as we wait?

5   'Wars, fighting, destruction, suffering, death' – pray as a group for these situations, and give thanks for the peacemakers.

NEW DAYLIGHT SUBSCRIPTION FORM

New Daylight and all our other Bible reading notes can be ordered
online at **brfonline.org.uk/collections/subscriptions**

☐ I would like to take out a subscription:

Title _____ First name/initials _____ Surname _____

Address _____

_____ Postcode _____

Telephone _____ Email _____

Please send *New Daylight* beginning with the January / May / September issue
(*delete as appropriate*) for the year 2021 / 2022 / 2023 (*delete as appropriate*):

(*please tick box*)	UK	Europe	Rest of world
New Daylight 1-year subscription	☐ £18.00	☐ £25.95	☐ £29.85
New Daylight 3-year subscription	☐ £52.65	N/A	N/A
New Daylight Deluxe	☐ £22.35	☐ £32.55	☐ £38.55

Total enclosed £ _____ (cheques should be made payable to 'BRF')

Prices valid until 30 April 2022. Please check **brfonline.org.uk** for current prices.

Please charge my MasterCard / Visa ☐ Debit card ☐ with £ _____

Card no. ☐☐☐☐ ☐☐☐☐ ☐☐☐☐ ☐☐☐☐

Expires end ☐☐☐☐   Security code* ☐☐☐   Last 3 digits on the reverse of the card

Signature* _____ Date _____ /_____ /_____
*ESSENTIAL IN ORDER TO PROCESS YOUR PAYMENT

To set up a Direct Debit, please visit **brfonline.org.uk/collections/subscriptions**.

Please return this form with the appropriate payment to:
BRF, 15 The Chambers, Vineyard, Abingdon OX14 3FE

To read our terms and find out about cancelling your order,
please visit **brfonline.org.uk/terms**.

BRF

Enabling all ages to grow in faith

Anna Chaplaincy
Living Faith
Messy Church
Parenting for Faith

The Bible Reading Fellowship (BRF) is a Christian charity that resources individuals and churches. Our vision is to enable people of all ages to grow in faith and understanding of the Bible and to see more people equipped to exercise their gifts in leadership and ministry.

To find out more about our ministries, visit

brf.org.uk